Simple Organisms

by Lisa Zamosky

Science Contributor
Sally Ride Science
Science Consultants
Thomas R. Ciccone, Science Educator
Ronald Edwards, Science Educator

MISSION: SCIENCE

Developed with contributions from Sally Ride Science™

Sally Ride Science™ is an innovative content company dedicated to fueling young people's interests in science.

Our publications and programs provide opportunities for students and teachers to explore the captivating world of science—from astrobiology to zoology.

We bring science to life and show young people that science is creative, collaborative, fascinating, and fun.

To learn more, visit www.SallyRideScience.com

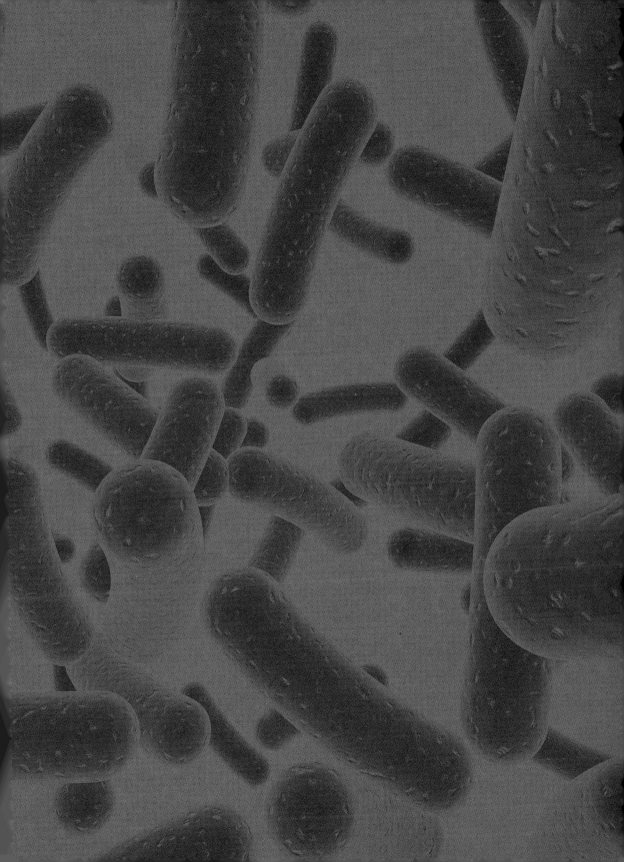

First hardcover edition published in 2009 by
Compass Point Books
151 Good Counsel Drive
P.O. Box 669
Mankato, MN 56002-0669

Editor: Brenda Haugen
Designer: Heidi Thompson
Editorial Contributor: Sue Vander Hook

Art Director: LuAnn Ascheman-Adams
Creative Director: Keith Griffin
Editorial Director: Nick Healy
Managing Editor: Catherine Neitge

 This book was manufactured with paper containing at least 10 percent post-consumer waste.

Library of Congress Cataloging-in-Publication Data
Zamosky, Lisa.
 Simple organisms / by Lisa Zamosky.
    p. cm. — (Mission: Science)
Includes index.
ISBN 978-0-7565-3955-9 (library binding)
1. Life (Biology)—Juvenile literature. 2. Organisms—Juvenile literature.
I. Title.
QH309.2.Z36 2009
579—dc22   2008007723

Visit Compass Point Books on the Internet at *www.compasspointbooks.com*
or e-mail your request to *custserv@compasspointbooks.com*

Table of Contents

The World of Microorganisms

Living organisms are all around you. Plants, animals, and fish are organisms, and so are you. But there are also trillions of tiny organisms you can see only with a microscope. Some of them, like bacteria, are made up of only one cell. They swarm throughout your body, swim in lakes and ponds, and float through the air.

In 1673, Dutch scientist Anton van Leeuwenhoek was the first to see these tiny microscopic beings. With his own homemade microscope, he observed a whole new world of living things. What he saw shocked him. In a drop of water were small creatures swimming around, organisms so small no one knew they existed.

Van Leeuwenhoek called them animacules. Today we call them microorganisms or microbes. The microorganisms van Leeuwenhoek discovered didn't fit into the plant or animal kingdoms that scientists were familiar with. Scientists have since divided microorganisms into four kingdoms: bacteria, archaea, protista, and fungi.

Scientists have not been able to count all the microorganisms on Earth. They continue to study this vast fascinating world of microscopic life.

Anton van Leeuwenhoek
(1632–1723)

Van Leeuwenhoek's Microscopes

Although van Leeuwenhoek didn't invent the microscope, he improved it significantly by making lenses with greater magnification. Over time, van Leeuwenhoek built more than 400 microscopes. Nine of his microscopes still exist.

Van Leeuwenhoek never taught his skill of making microscopes to anyone else. He didn't share his microscopes with others either.

For nearly 100 years, no one tried to duplicate or add to his work.

Van Leeuwenhoek often described and sketched what he saw under his microscopes. He told scholars and scientists about the bacteria in pond water and on people's teeth. At that time, most people didn't clean their teeth, so there were many creatures living there. Van Leeuwenhoek believed they made people's breath stink.

▲ Anton van Leeuwenhoek observed single-celled organisms under one of his own handcrafted microscopes.

◄ Scholars didn't trust van Leeuwenhoek when he first presented his drawings of single-celled organisms.

7

Organisms in the bacteria and archaea kingdoms thrive everywhere on Earth—in water, air, soil, and even under Earth's crust. They survive in very hot places as well as areas where temperatures drop below freezing.

Billions of bacteria make their homes in our bodies. Most of these tiny microbes are made up of a single cell with no nucleus—a group of microorganisms called prokaryotes. They swim in your digestive system and crawl around on your skin. More bacteria live in your colon than the total number of people who have ever lived. In fact, 95 percent of all your cells are bacteria that live mainly in your stomach and intestines. Your gut alone holds about 4 4/5 pounds (2 kilograms) of bacteria.

Archaea are similar to bacteria but have a different genetic makeup. Scientists once thought archaea lived only in extreme environments in the deepest parts of the sea. But now they know that archaea live in all habitats of Earth.

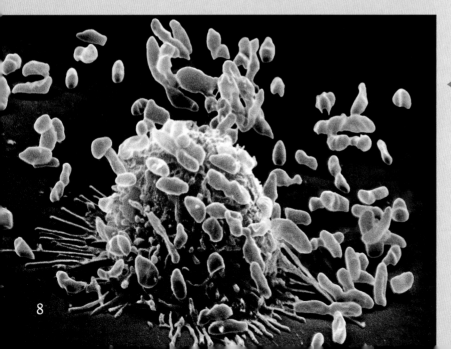

◀ Tiny bacteria (white cells)

Countless bacteria (yellow) live on the inner surface of the stomach. ▶

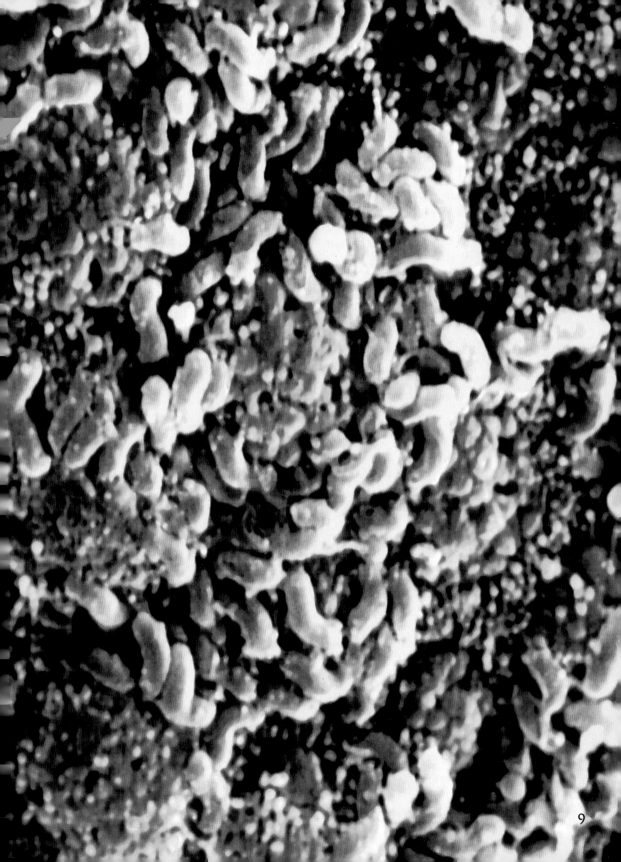

9

Bacteria come in three basic shapes—rods, globes, and spirals. Rod-shaped bacteria have flagella, or tiny hairs, that help them move from one place to another. Bacteria in the shape of globes group together in bunches like grapes. Spiral-shaped bacteria look like corkscrews and have flagella to get them from place to place.

Most bacteria are harmless and even beneficial. However, a few, called pathogenic bacteria, cause diseases such as strep, salmonella, E. coli, anthrax, and others.

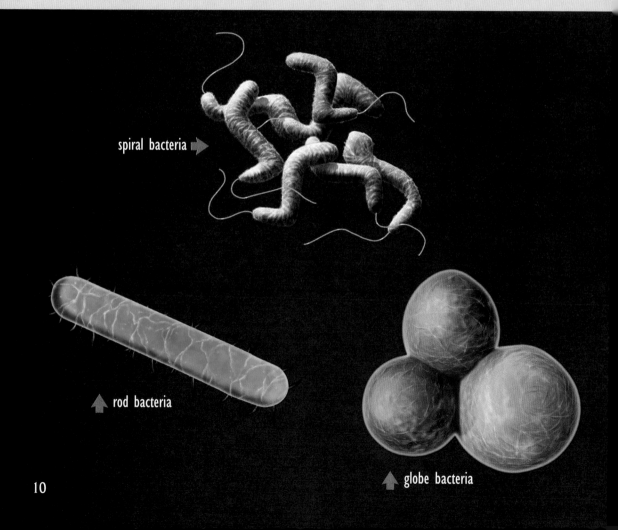

spiral bacteria ➡

⬆ rod bacteria

⬆ globe bacteria

Microbe Hunter

Rita Colwell is an environmental microbiologist. She hunts for harmful microbes. Colwell says, "I learn how microbes live in the environment, and how they can cause disease."

While working in India, Colwell learned that many people were getting sick from drinking water that had pathogenic microbes in it. First she discovered how the microbes got into the water, and then she taught people how to pour water through cloth before drinking it. The cloth captured the microbes, making the water safer to drink. Colwell once said, "I like making discoveries that help people stay healthy."

Colwell also looks for microbes in the ocean, using satellite pictures for clues. Dark spots or bright colors may indicate where large groups of microbes have gathered.

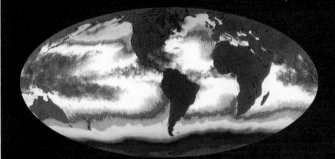

Patches of red and orange from a satellite image of Earth give clues to where microbes may be lurking.

Protista Kingdom

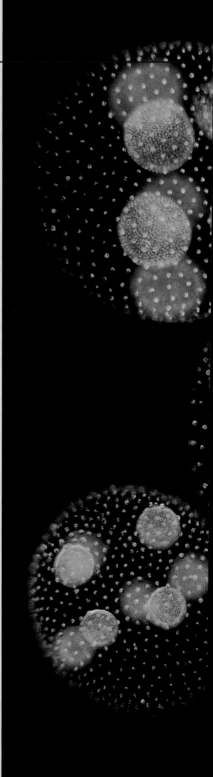

One-celled organisms in the Protista Kingdom are called protists. These eukaryotic cells have a nucleus, the cell's control center. Double membranes keep their complex structures enclosed and organized. They are much bigger than bacteria and archaea. They can also do things that the prokaryotes cannot.

Some protists group together to form colonies, working more efficiently side by side. The individual cells take in food and reproduce by dividing. Some protists make food from sunlight in a process called photosynthesis. Protists also use air and water to make food, releasing oxygen in the process. Together protists produce most of the oxygen we breathe.

Protists sometimes form colonies in ball shapes.

▲ Some protists link together in long strings that wave back and forth in water, allowing the colony to capture more sunlight.

Did You Know?

Scientists believe the first protist probably existed about 1.7 billion years ago.

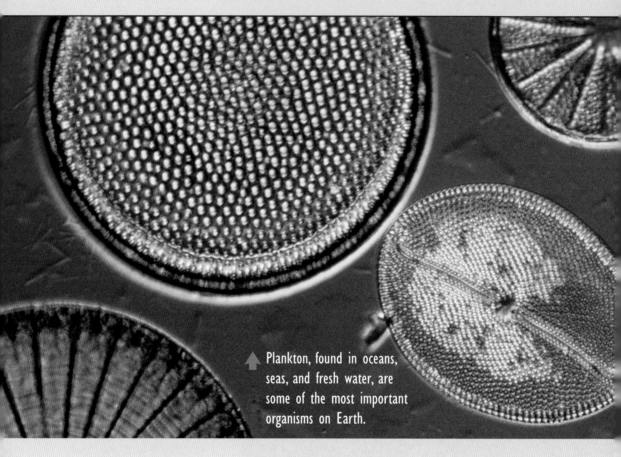

Plankton, found in oceans, seas, and fresh water, are some of the most important organisms on Earth.

Diatoms

In our oceans, seas, and fresh water live abundant supplies of plankton, the food for most underwater life. Shrimp, crabs, and countless other sea life eat plankton, an important part of the food chain.

Plankton are microorganisms called diatoms, a type of protist. There are more than 5,000 kinds of diatoms. They have outer shells made of silicon, the same thing used to make glass. Diatoms come in a variety of shapes and are often very beautiful. They can be oval, round, or leaf-shaped. Some diatoms look like commas, and others look like periods.

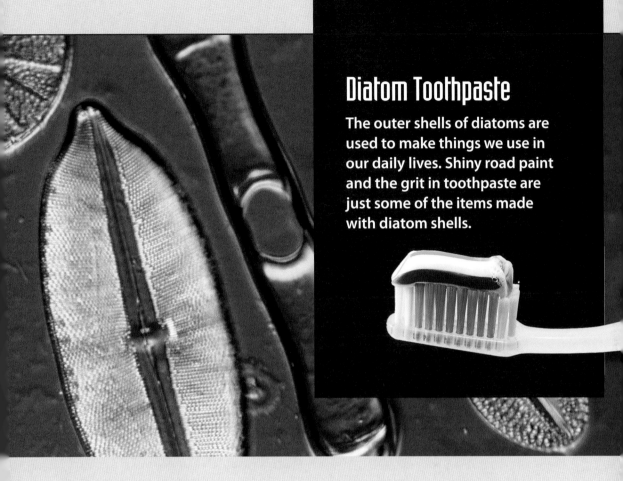

Diatom Toothpaste

The outer shells of diatoms are used to make things we use in our daily lives. Shiny road paint and the grit in toothpaste are just some of the items made with diatom shells.

Diatoms have a top and a bottom shell. A diatom reproduces when these shells divide. The contents of the cell divide between the two parts. Then each part grows another half to become a whole. The new diatom produced by the smaller bottom shell is smaller than the original diatom. After many cell divisions, shells produced from the bottom shell may become too small to hold the contents of the cell. When this happens, the diatom either dies or leaves its shell and becomes a spore.

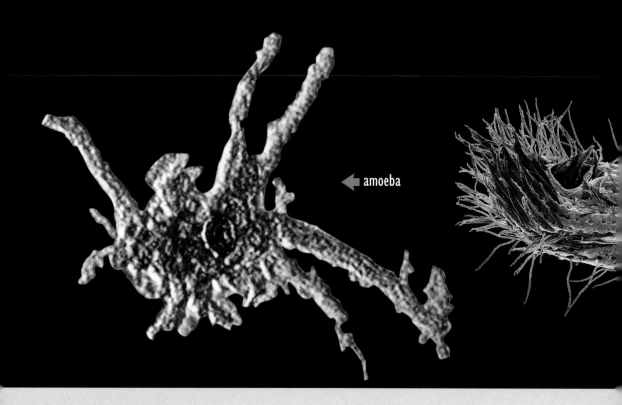

amoeba

Protozoa

Protists that behave like little animals are called protozoa. They move around, hunt other microbes for food, and eat lots of bacteria. There are more protozoa in the world than any other kind of organism.

These single-celled organisms take in food through the tissues of their cells and through pores. Once protozoa digest their food, they give off nitrogen, a gas that other plants and animals need in order to live.

Protozoa fall into three categories: amoebas, ciliates (the largest group), and flagellates (the smallest group).

flagellate

ciliate

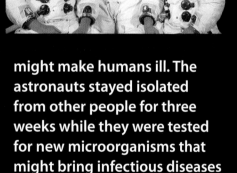

Lunar Quarantine

On July 20, 1969, the *Apollo 11* astronauts landed on the moon. They spent 22 hours there, taking rock samples and making observations. Three days later, they returned to Earth and were immediately put in quarantine.

No one knew what "moon germs" or undiscovered microbes they might have brought back with them that might make humans ill. The astronauts stayed isolated from other people for three weeks while they were tested for new microorganisms that might bring infectious diseases to Earth.

On August 13, 1969, the astronauts were released from quarantine with a clean bill of health.

17

Amoebas

One of the simplest protozoa is an amoeba, about as big as the head of a pin. Amoebas live in rivers and ponds. They also can be found on leaves of plants that live in water. These one-celled organisms eat, give off waste products, and reproduce by dividing.

An amoeba is made of liquid and held together by an outer membrane. It moves around by changing shape and sticking out a projection called a pseudopod, or false foot. In the middle of the amoeba is a floating nucleus, the amoeba's control center.

Amoebas take in water, oxygen, and food through tiny holes in their cell membranes. An amoeba reproduces by first dividing its nucleus and then separating into two parts. If the cell were to split before the nucleus did, the half without the nucleus would die.

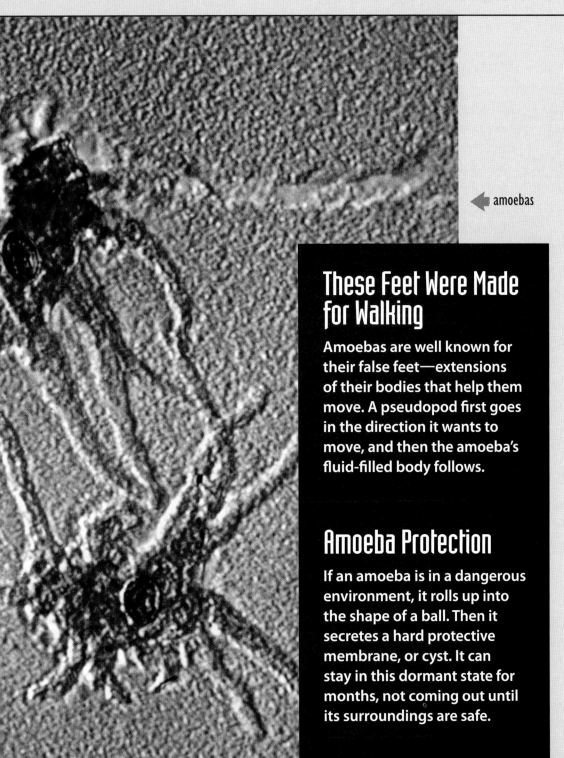

amoebas

These Feet Were Made for Walking

Amoebas are well known for their false feet—extensions of their bodies that help them move. A pseudopod first goes in the direction it wants to move, and then the amoeba's fluid-filled body follows.

Amoeba Protection

If an amoeba is in a dangerous environment, it rolls up into the shape of a ball. Then it secretes a hard protective membrane, or cyst. It can stay in this dormant state for months, not coming out until its surroundings are safe.

19

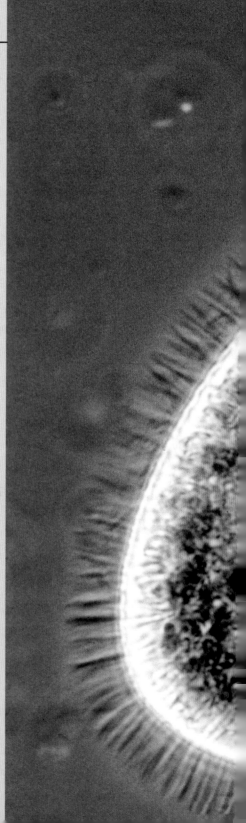

Ciliates

Ciliates are the largest protozoa, but these simple organisms can move very quickly. Their speed comes from cilia, short hairlike structures that look like eyelashes. These cilia are constantly moving, working like tiny oars to move ciliates quickly through the water.

There are more than 8,000 types of ciliates. Scientists believe there are even more that haven't yet been discovered. Ciliates live in every type of water—oceans, lakes, ponds, rivers, and even damp soil. Most ciliates feed on smaller organisms such as bacteria. They can be found in places where natural things have started to rot. In fact, most ciliates live in water with rotting plants and protists.

Ciliates, the largest of the protozoa, are characterized by short hairlike cilia.

Ciliate Protection

When the environment becomes harsh, ciliates become smaller and enclose themselves in a protective sac. When conditions improve, the sac opens up, and the ciliate emerges to feed and reproduce.

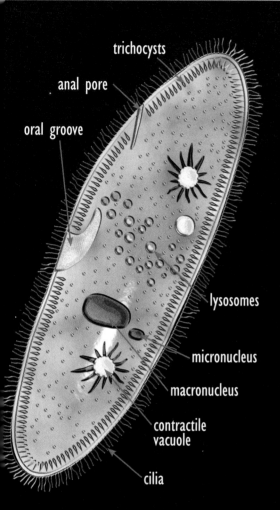

trichocysts

anal pore

oral groove

lysosomes

micronucleus

macronucleus

contractile
vacuole

cilia

Complex Creatures?

Paramecia are complex organisms that can detect extreme temperatures and chemicals and move away from them. If they eat something they don't like, they will stay away from it the next time.

The most common ciliate is the paramecium, which can be seen with the naked eye. Paramecia live in fresh water and look like tiny gray specks on the surface. They are commonly found in scummy water, where they feed on bacteria and other small cells.

A paramecium has some interesting parts. About halfway down one side is its oral groove where cilia sweep food into the cell. At each end of its long body is a star-shaped vacuole that acts as a storage chamber. Vacuoles also pump out unneeded water and waste to prevent the paramecium from filling up too much and bursting. A paramecium also has rodlike structures called trichocysts that give it shape and hold food in place while the cell digests it. Paramecia reproduce by cell division, first splitting in two, then becoming four, eight, and so on.

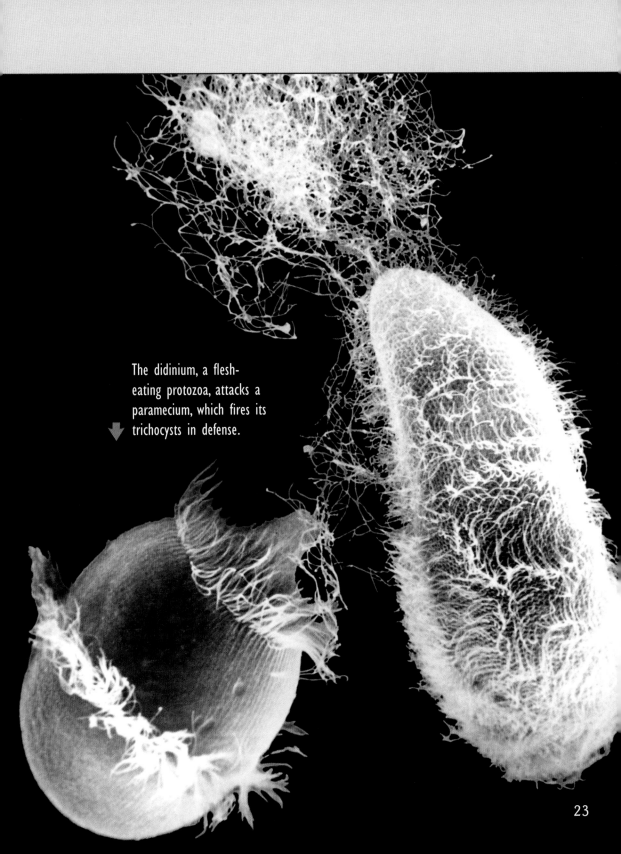

The didinium, a flesh-
eating protozoa, attacks a
paramecium, which fires its
trichocysts in defense.

Fungi Kingdom

The fourth kingdom of microorganisms is the Fungi Kingdom. Examples of fungi include mushrooms, molds, and yeast. Scientists once thought fungi were organisms like plants, but then they discovered fungi acted more like animals. They don't make their own food like plants do. In fact, they digest their food outside their bodies through their cell walls.

Fungi come in many shapes and sizes. Some fungi such as yeast are single-celled organisms. One yeast cell is too small to see without a microscope. But when yeast cells gather into a cluster, they can be seen on fruit or leaves. They look like a white powdery coating.

Multicelled fungi such as mold live in clusters and are found almost everywhere. Fungi reproduce in two ways—they form spores that wind and rain carry away, or they reproduce by growing hyphae. These long branching cells bud at the tip of a fungus cell and form a long threadlike chain of cells. The fuzzy appearance of mold is created by long strands of hyphae.

Hyphae cells give mold its fuzzy appearance.

Important Discoveries

French scientist Louis Pasteur spent most of his life studying microbes that cause disease. In his experiments with yeast, he found two types. One was useful for making foods such as yogurt and wine, and the other turned food sour. Pasteur found that heating wine or milk killed most of the bacteria and mold as well as the "bad" yeast that turned them sour. This process, which is still used today, is called pasteurization, named for Louis Pasteur.

▲ Louis Pasteur (1822—1895)

Treating Disease With Bacteria

In the late 1970s, a team of scientists found that bacteria could be used to make insulin. For many years, insulin from animals had been used to treat diabetes, but some people were allergic to it. Scientists found they could genetically engineer bacteria called E. coli to make synthetic human insulin.

25

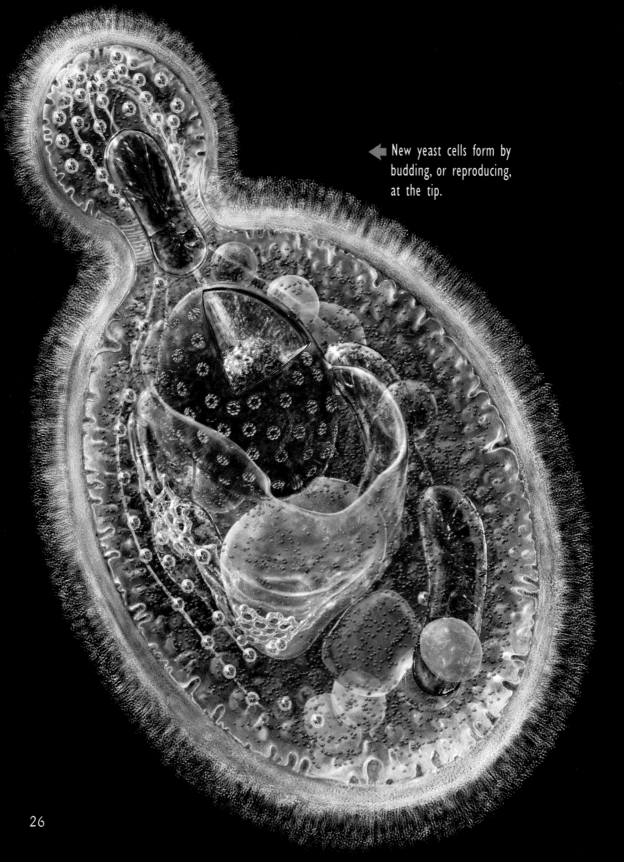

New yeast cells form by budding, or reproducing, at the tip.

Certain fungi perform an important role in our world. Several types of fungi are used to make important antibiotics that fight bacterial infections. Fungi also naturally produce substances in our bodies that fight harmful bacteria. Other fungi, such as baker's yeast, are used to make bread rise and brew beer.

All fungi are not beneficial, however. Certain types of fungi are dangerous and can cause serious diseases in plants, animals, and humans. Fungi ruin parts of fruit and vegetable crops each year.

Mushrooms and toadstools are types of fungi.

Fungi, Fungi Everywhere

One teaspoon of topsoil contains about 120,000 fungi. Fungi can survive in almost any environment, including places with very low moisture. Mold, a type of fungus, is found in oceans and ponds as well as on plants and animals and in our homes.

Baker's yeast makes bread dough rise.

Microorganisms will always be a part of our world. They are in our water, in the atmosphere, in underground rocks, and inside our bodies. Most microbes keep our environment clean and help us stay healthy.

Vaccine for Bird Flu

In 2007, the U.S. Food and Drug Administration approved the first vaccine for humans against H5N1, the avian flu virus. Commonly known as the bird flu, this virus is mainly an animal disease. But about 300 people in the world have been infected with it since 2003. About half of them died. There have been no cases of bird flu in humans in the United States. Scientists developed the H5N1 vaccine in case this virus spreads to a large number of people.

But when pathogenic bacteria threaten to make us sick, our bodies fight back. Usually the body's natural defenses kill harmful bacteria or stop them from reproducing. But sometimes we need help from antibiotics prescribed by a doctor.

Microbes are important to our existence. Scientists continue to study these simple organisms that can only be seen through a microscope. They learn how microorganisms benefit humans. Scientists also hunt for new strains of bacteria or viruses that threaten to harm us. They are constantly testing and developing new antibiotics and vaccines that will fight and destroy harmful microorganisms.

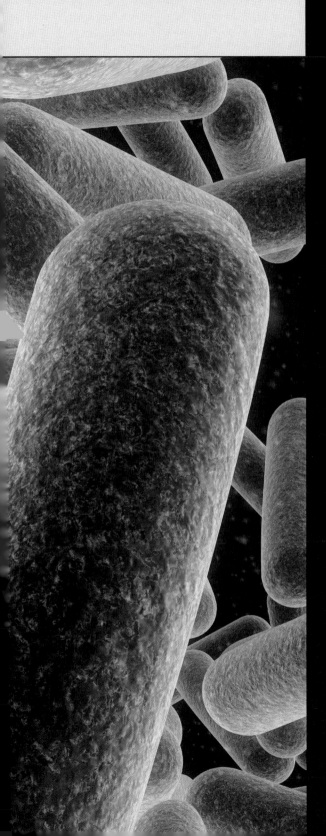

Wash Your Hands

About 100,000 microbes live on every half-inch square of your skin. Most of them are harmless, but some of them—germs—could make you sick. Germs on your hands are most likely to enter your mouth or nose. Washing your hands for 15 seconds with soap and water will kill most germs.

Joseph Lister (1827–1912) was a British surgeon who was the first doctor to clean his hands and surgical instruments before an operation. Before the mid-1900s, more people in hospitals died from infection than from the operation they were undergoing. Surgeons reused bloody instruments and seldom washed their hands. Today everyone in an operating room scrubs their hands with soap for five minutes, and all surgical tools are sterilized.

In this experiment, you and your partner will test how effective hand washing is in preventing the spread of germs.

Materials

- chart paper
- colored markers
- apron or smock
- washable paint
- timer or watch
- sink
- blindfold
- towels
- soap

Procedure

1. Divide a sheet of paper into four sections with a marker. Draw an outline of a hand in each section. Shade in your idea of hands that look completely dirty, very dirty, dirty, and a little dirty. Label each section. Now create two scoring charts, one labeled "Water" and the other "Water and Soap."

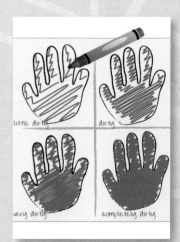

2   Choose one person to be the hand washer and another to be the timekeeper.

3   Thoroughly cover the hand washer's hands with washable paint and let the paint dry completely.

4   Go to the sink and put a blindfold on the hand washer. The washer should run his or her hands under running water for one second. The timekeeper should dry the hand washer's hands by lightly touching a towel to the skin (do not rub off the paint). Compare the washer's hands with the chart. On the Water scoring chart, record how clean the washer's hands are.

5   Now the washer should wash his or her hands with water for four more seconds. Again the timekeeper should lightly blot the washer's hands. Record on the Water scoring chart how clean the hands are.

6 The washer should now wash with water for 15 seconds. Blot with a towel and record the cleanliness on the chart.

7 Take the blindfold off. Allow the washer to completely clean his or her hands with water. Repeat steps 3 through 6, but this time the washer should use soap and water for each step. Use the Water and Soap scoring chart to record how clean the washer's hands are after each washing.

8 Change roles. Repeat the activity until everyone has had a turn as the hand washer.

9 Display your results. Create two graphs showing the average cleanliness score at each washing step. One graph will show the results when using water only. The other graph will show results when using water and soap.

Ferdinand Cohn (1828–1898)
German biologist who is considered one of the founders
of microbiology; classified bacteria as plants and divided
bacteria into four groups

Casimir Davaine (1812–1882)
French physician and microbiologist who discovered the
anthrax bacterium and showed how it is passed on from
one animal to another

Robert Hooke (1635–1703)
English scientist credited with observing the first
cells under a microscope and naming them *cellulae*
(cells); drew detailed images of his observations
using a microscope and published them in 1665 in his
book *Micrographia*

Robert Koch (1843–1910)
German physician who was awarded the Nobel Prize in
medicine for his discovery of the tuberculosis bacterium;
considered one of the founders of microbiology

Louis Pasteur (1822–1895)
French scientist who is considered one of the founders
of microbiology and known for his breakthroughs in
disease prevention; developed the first vaccine for rabies
and created pasteurization, a method to prevent milk
and wine from souring

Anton van Leeuwenhoek (1632–1723)
Dutch scientist who made hundreds of microscopes
and observed bacteria cells for the first time; commonly
known as the father of microbiology

Glossary

amoeba—single-celled organism that has no definite form and moves by means of pseudopods

antibiotics—substances made from certain fungi or bacteria that can destroy or weaken microorganisms that cause infections or diseases

bacteria—one-celled organisms that do not have a nucleus and sometimes cause disease

cell—basic unit of life

cilia—microscopic hairlike projections on the surfaces of some cells

ciliates—class of protozoans with short hairlike appendages extending from their surfaces

diatom—microscopic one-celled protist that lives in marine or fresh water and often lives in colonies

digest—convert food into absorbable substances

flagella—long, threadlike appendages, usually with a whiplike action that helps the organism move

flagellates—protozoans that move by means of flagella

fungi—organisms that reproduce by spores and include molds, mildews, yeast, and mushrooms

hyphae—long, branchlike strands of fungi

insulin—hormone produced by the pancreas and necessary for glucose to enter body cells

kingdom—category into which natural organisms and objects are classified

membrane—thin, flexible layer of tissue that covers the surface or separates regions of an organism

microbe—tiny life form, especially a bacterium that causes disease

microorganism—organism that is too small to see

microscope—instrument that uses a lens or lenses to magnify very small objects

microscopic—too small to be seen by the unaided eye but large enough to be seen with a microscope

mold—type of fungus that causes organic matter to break down

nucleus—part of the cell that controls its behavior

organism—living thing or system

paramecium—freshwater ciliate protozoan that is characteristically slipper-shaped and covered with cilia

pasteurization—process of heating a liquid or food in order to kill microorganisms that could cause disease, spoiling, or unwanted fermentation

photosynthesis—process by which green plants make their food

plankton—small or microscopic organisms that float or drift in great numbers in fresh or salt water

pore—tiny opening in a skin or membrane

protozoa—large group of single-celled, usually microscopic organisms

quarantine—period of time during which a person, animal, or object that may carry a disease is kept in isolation so the disease cannot spread

reproduce—create offspring

species—single distinct class of living creature with features that set it apart from others

spore—single-celled reproductive body that grows into a new organism

trichocysts—rodlike structures in the body of a paramecium

vacuole—hollow space in the cytoplasm of a cell

yeast—type of fungi

1665	Robert Hooke views cell structure of cork under a microscope
1683	Anton van Leeuwenhoek discovers living bacteria in pond water and on teeth
1831	Robert Brown reports his discovery of the nucleus, the command center of the cell
1838	Matthias Schleiden finds that plants are made up of cells
1844	Karl Nägeli sees the process of cell growth and division under a microscope
1850	French physician Casimir Davaine and French dermatologist Pierre François Olive Rayer discover the anthrax bacterium in the blood of diseased sheep
1853	Louis Pasteur is awarded the French Legion of Honor
1855	Rudolf Virchow states that all living cells come from other living cells
1870	Pasteur and Robert Koch establish that certain microorganisms, or germs, are the cause of many diseases
1881	Pasteur develops a vaccine for anthrax
1882	Pasteur develops a vaccine for rabies; Walther Flemming publishes a book that illustrates and describes cell division; Koch discovers the bacterium responsible for tuberculosis, for which he receives the Nobel Prize in medicine
1890	Emil von Behring uses antitoxins to make tetanus and diphtheria vaccines

1921	Frederick Banting and Charles Best discover insulin is important for the treatment of diabetes
1923	First vaccine for diphtheria is developed
1926	First vaccine for pertussis is developed
1927	First vaccine for tetanus is developed
1928	Alexander Fleming discovers penicillin
1935	First vaccine for yellow fever is developed
1952	Jonas Salk develops the first polio vaccine
1962	First oral polio vaccine is used
1964	First vaccine for measles is developed
1967	First vaccines for mumps and smallpox are developed
1970	First vaccine for rubella is developed
1981	First vaccine for hepatitis B is developed
1995	First vaccine for chickenpox is developed
2003	Carlo Urbani of Doctors Without Borders alerts the World Health Organization about the SARS virus, resulting in the most effective response to an epidemic in history; Urbani dies of the disease in less than a month
2007	The U.S. Food and Drug Administration approves the first vaccine for humans against the avian influenza virus H5N1
2008	U.S. Centers for Disease Control and Prevention conducts a study to find out if exposure to a preservative in vaccines in infancy is related to the development of autism

Additional Resources

Anderson, Rodney P. *The Invisible ABCs*. Washington, D.C.:
     ASM Press, 2007.

Brunelle, Lynn. *Bacteria*. Milwaukee: Gareth Stevens
     Publishing, 2004.

Claybourne, Anna. *Microlife: From Amoebas to Viruses*.
     Chicago: Heinemann Library, 2004.

Fandel, Jennifer. *Louis Pasteur and Pasteurization*. Mankato,
     Minn.: Capstone Press, 2007.

Pascoe, Elaine. *Single-Celled Organisms*. New York: PowerKids
     Press, 2003.

On the Web

For more information on this topic,
use FactHound.

1. Go to *www.facthound.com*

2. Type in this book ID: 0756539552

3. Click on the *Fetch It* button.

FactHound will find the best
Web sites for you.

Index

About the Author

Lisa Zamosky

Lisa Zamosky earned her master's degree from the University of Southern California and worked in the health care field in New York City for more than 10 years before becoming a freelance writer. Zamosky has written more than 40 books for the education market. She also writes articles involving scientific and medical research, covering medicine, pharmaceuticals, biotechnology, fitness, nutrition, and the health care system for consumer and business magazines, both in print and on the Web. Zamosky lives in Southern California with her husband and son.

Image Credits